I0819559

Joyful Books for Curious Minds

An imprint of Macmillan Children's Publishing Group, LLC
Odd Dot® is a registered trademark of Macmillan Publishing Group, LLC.
120 Broadway, New York, NY 10271
OddDot.com • mackids.com

EU representative: Macmillan Publishers Ireland Ltd, 1st Floor,
The Liffey Trust Centre, 117–126 Sheriff Street Upper, Dublin 1, DO1 YC43

EDITOR Kate Avino
DESIGNER Mariam Quraishi
PRODUCTION EDITOR Mia Moran
PRODUCTION MANAGER Jocelyn O'Dowd

Library of Congress Control Number: 2025944635
ISBN 978-1-250-37981-8

This work is an independent biography and is not authorized, sponsored, or endorsed by Dwayne "The Rock" Johnson.

First edition, 2026
Printed in China by RR Donnelley Asia Printing Solutions Ltd., Dongguan City, Guangdong Province

1 3 5 7 9 10 8 6 4 2

A Book for the Littlest Dwayne "The Rock" Johnson Fans

You Are STRONG

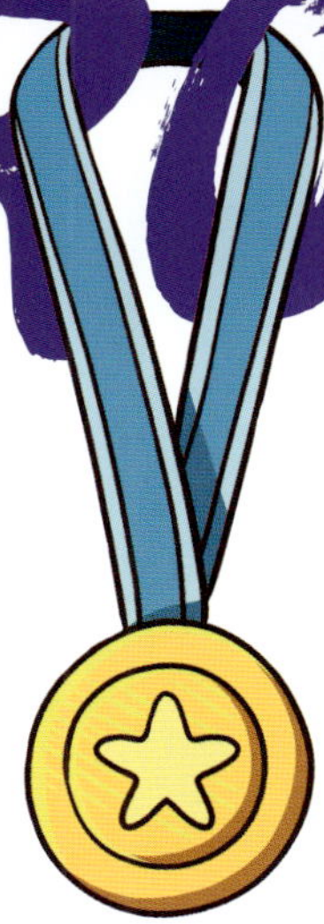

illustrated by Loilufy

New York

You are strong, baby.

A force of nature,

an embodiment of the
aloha spirit.

ou R The #1
02
07

You tackle every challenge

with resilience

and an unbreakable will.

You rock the world, baby.

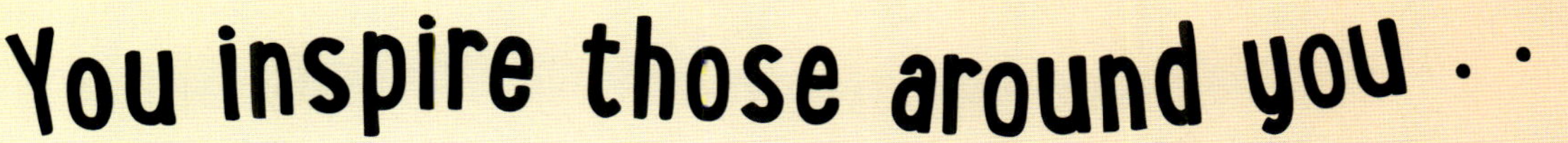

You inspire those around you . . .

. . . as you create
your own path.
PRODUCTION:
DATE
2001
SCENE
OUT

Guided by ambition
and driven to prove your ability.

you are the superhero

of your own story.

And you are destined for many adventures!

You harness your own mana, baby,

and the world awaits
your legacy!